Bad Star

Rebecca Hazelton

YesYes Books Portland Oregon

Copyright © 2013 by Rebecca Hazelton

Cover Art: "Ebb Series (8)" © 2013 by Exit Deer
Cover Design by Alban Fischer
Book Design by KMA Sullivan

All rights reserved. No part of this book may be reproduced without the publisher's written permission, except for brief quotations for reviews.

First Edition, 2013
ISBN: 978-1-936919-24-6
Printed in the United States of America

Published by YesYes Books
1232 NE Prescott Street
Portland, OR 97211
YesYesBooks.com

For a bad star by which I sailed

Table of Events

1. The places lovers meet encode in the body: the lake and the bench beside, the car and the pacing road, the zoo where the lone bear won't come out from the cave.

2. The cord around a lover's wrist tells us to remember.

3. With a practiced motion, he pulls her arm back and she, in a rehearsed way, lets her eyes roll up. They listen to her exhale.

4. In the foreground, one man puts his hands around another man's throat. In the background, one man puts his hands around another man's throat.

5. One tiger falls on another tiger. One elephant tramples another.

6. The cord around a lover's neck and the hand that leads the leash.

7. The script calls for a brutal fight. The actors are trained in feigning violence. She is trained to observe and pulse accordingly.

8. The second man is very still. He deserves what he deserves.

9. The deer sniffs the fallen doe. Get up.

10. He holds his thumb to the pulse in her neck, presses. *I could make you lose consciousness*, he said. *I could do that.*

11. If she unties the knot then who remembers? If she ties it to another animal and walks that animal down another set of roads.

12 The bench is empty. The lake empties of fish.

13 High up in the tree, he can't see her body, just the fruit she tosses down.

14 A wadded piece of red silk, damp from the tongue.

15 The knife in her hand for the fruit. One animal to another.

16 Cutting is the fastest way to untie, the surest.

MAKE GOOD

Promise me there is an end
                         to this ever. Promise me the tulips that return
with black centers and lurid pollen
                         will waste and wither in the heat.
Promise me this Tom Collins glass
                         will sweat itself out. Promise me another.
Promise me another kiss
                         to my forehead, a sweating goodbye,

promise me you won't
                         come back. Promise me the rabbits
will starve in their burrows.
                         Promise me the rain coming down.
                                       Promise me the fox kits will drown.

Promise me a house a car a gate
                         a small dog to wag when I come home.
Promise me a mailbox with my name on it.
                         Promise me a new name that suits me.
Promise me the dog won't die.
                         Promise me a mouse in the pantry and small droppings
                         in the food.
                         Promise me moths in the clothes,
the small holes that grow larger.
                         Promise me your hands tied
                                       behind your back.
Promise me we'll laugh and laugh.

Promise me a child will shake out like pollen from a tulip.
                                        Promise me you aren't the man you promised.
Promise me that the hands I cut off and buried
                      in the backyard were my hands.
Promise me they won't grow back.

NOT ATLANTA OR ATALANTA

She's not a gate left unlatched.
The garden is not one
        where the tree branches brush the ground
because the fruit is so heavy,
        and she's not that rotting sweetness
        or that fermented juice,
        she's not the monkeys
pawing it to their mouths
        or their drunken stumbling after.
She is not a golden apple
        or the lust for possession.
She's not the foot race that ends with her married off,
        and she's not the lion skin she wears
because proper thanks were forgotten.
        She thanks.
        She thanks the wedding guests
        who brought so many presents.
The vacuum that never loses suction.
The immersion blender.
The golden apple rolling down the aisle.
The ships
that crowd the shore.
The men
who tear her away
and the man who tosses her over one broad shoulder.
She is not the beauty this implies.
        She's not a face that slips
        the ships from dock.

She doesn't race after an apple
                for knowledge but would to forget.
                She does not apple, ever.
She's not Peachtree Street or Peachtree Street or Peachtree Street.
                She's not the Majestic
                              serving food that pleases.
She does not please.

DESTROY, SHE SAID

She wears the Mason Dixon line
                        on her ring finger,
and the pale skin
           beneath
        measures the time she's spent
                        sequestered
     in a grow-house
            under cloudy glass.

How long until the man
       who reads the poem
reads himself into the
                space, the cleft, the #s
she texts out
     to the universe?

The world
            on her tongue
like a lozenge slick
        and melting,
and when finally
        the hurt is soothed
        it's the pain of it she'll miss,
the shimmering thing she kept longest.

BEFORE SHE RINGS HIS DOOR

She is shameless for a moment,
       though shame will follow, and feels joy—
having walked a mile in deep snow
               past the aging townhomes,
past the community garden
          blasted by frost, the kiosk pinned with years
                   of messages, apartments for let,
                   bands to form, lost
                         and wanted,
the frozen lake that could support a woman, a man,
             and the weight of their proximity,
past even the idea of herself as a woman walking
           to her own sadness,
a thing that she feels distantly
           inside her, raising its weak wings, hissing
like the injured goose she sees in the snow, his companions
                        long gone,
keenly hearing
     the summer calling him home.

TRY VIOLENCE

The cord around a lover's wrist
tells her to remember. The red passion, the braid
overlap of one body to another. Knot to knot,
mouth to mouth, no one doubts anymore.
She wears it rather than red the wrist otherwise.
She read there was a cord from one dream
to another, that the dreamers might meet
while walking down the twist of thread.
She has worn and worn it down. The memory
reforms from stray fibers. Symbols are easy.
Harder his mouth to her ear, the promise
of further cruelty, how her heart sang
at the mention of her own breakage.
It was one room with poor lighting,
and in it they had some measure
of their shadows. The city around them
took up her cry and echoed it in siren,
a volley of distress. He left a mark
on her wrist. She wears it to remember.

PLAUSIBLE DENIAL

In beginnings there is a pleasure,
                    in the pleasure that begins
there is a beginning unpetaling
                    into thin color slips
                    plastering the car windshields,
                    blowing across the sidewalks,
where the pedestrians stroll sometimes
        hand in hand,
        and in all those tight buds unraveled
there is an order brought low,
    a previous destroyed,
because seeing a lover naked the first time
                    erases the previous
                    lover's body of any certainty
                    in your mind—
    where was that freckle,
    how high the breast—

I cannot remember how he kissed me,
        and though he slapped me
                when necessary, and in the face
            when I asked, I can't say anymore
            the size of his hands or
                    how the peace that settled over both of us.
His handprint
            was beginning to fade
                  as another beginning began,

      begun in the recoil
            of my head and my smile
in the anteroom
            of the previous ending,
and if the red thread
            I thought linked us abraded, snapped, or just faded
            it also knit into another's,
                      and then an other's,
so that in this night
      that I make new the old is unraveled and respun,
      in this night that makes me anew
            the old self is made stranger,

how can I
      deny her
      the requested blow,
            that she asked for,
                      that I asked for?

THE WORLD GROWS LARGER

After the kiss, he leans his forearm
against her throat,
              he fists her wrists into the sheets,
small violences
which swoon her silent
      and unafraid,

              nothing compared
        to the larger ones
less marking, where she wakes
and the room is empty
              but everywhere
is his presence, her hands
                carry his scent for days—

what joy,
      to feel opened up
           to wonder, to the approaching
      haunt of loss,

to have the real
           fear at last.

SELF PORTRAIT WITH UNSEWN SHADOW

See me as a boy in the window, never pleasing,
see me as the housebreaker, picklock, sick
with longing to steal
               you from your bedroom.
When my eyes cry that's salt…
               but I don't. When you cry
it's blackmail, it's girlhood, it's a plan.

How did you brother the others, how did you button
the fierce right out? When you shut the window
it's the worst sort of adventure.
O Darling, love as I knew it
was a savage straddling me, or a wife, a wife, a wife.

TWO MEN

Two men are explaining the world to each other.
One uses his hands. One uses the words
he uses for everything he needs. It's day
and the light has for them traveled
very far. One man gestures to the other to explain
how one creature might use another
to survive. Sea lice, for instance. Lamprey eels.
What about viruses, he signs,
what about a crystalline structure keyed
to wreak havoc in the brain? A deer
you slew with your father's bow might return
years later to riddle your memory with holes.
He gesticulates and his arms mimic a serpent
draped over the branch of a tree. But that's no
parasite. The man with the words considers.
He wants to say something about mythology.
How the deer might have been a god
and there is punishment written in the margins
of the world in a small and cramped script.
About how there might be a prohibition
against eating something you didn't kill,
at least, not with your own hands. He says it.
The man who speaks with his hands puts his
around the other man's neck. Like this?
He tightens. It feels right.
There aren't words for it so the other just nods.

SELF PORTRAIT AS THING IN THE FOREST

Behind this dress,
           two women
     in the mess of one body hardly covered
              by the stiff beauty of lustrous rustle.

Behind these freckled breasts,
           two hearts that rush the blood,
divergent desires—

     twin to the unseemly split between predator
                    and prey,
the white pet-store rat
     bred for the boa
              and the boa that would remake
the Florida landscape in his ever expanding image—

     if the one woman is the call
to the other's answer,
     the answer is to keep calling and calling
into the swamp and humid.
              If the container can't lull
     its contents into some sense of contentment,
the glass breaks, and out rush the teeth.

     In a fixed loop, tie this sash of silk shot, plain weave,
          and with a half hitch secure
against a hunger

    that grows without natural enemy.
A desire uncurbed
    is a flagrant thing, is a woman
      in the mirror, seeing clearly.

SOME SURPRISE

O, to be right and ratified
        in the universe's accident, to be a bright star
                in the wrong constellation,
      a shrug and a whatever,
                    the intended mercy
                    catch and release
                    of the speckled trout
                    trailing blood in the water
                    for any hungry thing to follow.

To recognize the delight in lying down,
        in watching the golden youth
                paraded through the town on weaker shoulders,
to see yourself
        in his face years prior
                and in the faces of those carrying him,
and in the faces of those walking away, tired.

DO NOT WANT

What the sky had to say in the dark thirty tune
            that the birds took up and V'd further,
or what the church bells pealed
                and repealed as commandment
to gather or pray or resign.
            The prints on my skin
            that were yours, were mine,
the bruises you left
on my arm,
            the satisfaction in harm for the asking
            or the gendarme you presented
when a man
with a lance was needed.

What the radio stuttered
what the front seat leaned
what the hand
in the crux of it faltered.
                Or the sense of myself
as a woman in a dress or the sense of myself
                unaltered or the sense of myself.
What the porch light saw
            what the neighbors knew
what the dog howled out
        to the street.
What a man felt in his fist when another man
            fell to his knees and the please of that sickening thump.

When my doorbell rang when all the doorbells rang
                in the hallway the building the man who was ringing
only wanted the woman to answer.
When I answered
           the door I was not the woman
                       he wanted the woman he wanted
                                    was hiding.
What he had to say to the dog that was barking
what she had to say to the uniformed men
what I had to say when you arrived and you held me
because I was fearful of the man
           of her fear of the fear that I'd be her
if you were a different man
                     which eventually you were.

DOMINION

Maybe the light from the window is yours.
                              Certainly the bed
                              is a possession.
      Certainly these sheets
              are districted and bordered,
                        the imprint of a body,
          maybe it is your body,
                          within the bounds of your sway
and measured and cordoned,
              accordingly,
and the birds and the fish,
          these are yours,
                  and that which crawls,
                            and that which pulls itself from the waters
and gasps on the shore,
          new to the sky's gray curve,
yours also,
          and the trees when they betray the wind
and the wind when it betrays the leaves,
                  and so much
gives another away
          in this world and that's yours
                        as well,
      your name is yours
                and all you can see,
                      you own it, so own it.

HOW DAMAGED

Like when waking to the wreckage is as easy as stretching
                out across the bed and feeling the warmth
        leaving the cooling depression—that knowledge
that no one is coming back, and no one wants to—
yes, that way,
                      where you are the leaving
                          and the left,
        the weft in the sheets
      ladder to the sunlight's weave
              the same as ever.

As if sex were a motion that slipped ships from docks
                    and Helen just one more woman
            shaped like an excuse.
Walls fall,
        but then, walls do
and afterwards, the sky looks broader,
      the horses on the horizon
                full of possibility.

FILM IN WHICH I AM A GOVERNESS IN YOUR HOUSE

By act three, we are a threesome,
 you, myself, and the awkward
space between us,
 that sometimes looks like our arms, seconded
 and ghostly, linked,
though sometimes your ghost arm
 has a small blade
 and is trying to saw
your other ghost arm
 loose from mine.
 These things aren't real,
I tell the children,
 do not be alarmed.
 It's unclear if we are
in a gothic tale
 in which there is a supernatural element
or if it's just
 that the house is poorly lit and there are secret
passageways and disguises and maybe their mother is alive—
 I don't know—but it's a rational universe
and the house is the same size inside
 as it is out.
What then,
 is to be the color
of our communications? Is every kiss
 we haven't yet shared
 to be negotiated

through correspondence passed
>from housekeeper to chambermaid to the chambermaid's
lover who mucks out the stables and places
>your soiled note in the pommel
of the saddled horse you've loaned me,
>because every woman should feel
>something powerful between her legs—you said that—
I wonder sometimes
>if you are the gentleman
I took you for,
>if in answering your advertisement
for a good woman
>to work for a good master
>we both falsified our character.

YOU MAKE ME TOUCH YOUR HANDS FOR STUPID REASONS

The air is the same
                as when three-toed horses
walked the earth, tender on the rocks.
The river interrupts the land, and the black dots
                on the hillside, the far away
    or the tiny, might be people,
might be ruptured
protein in the eyes' reversed image.
                Where are you?
          Sleeping, I am as I left myself
                but without my ID. I cannot find my shoes.
This happens when my nerves mistake
    the left for the ceiling, when I grow new skin
in response to the Midwest's unending horizon.
    There was something you were holding carefully.
Please feel free to imagine
          a standard baby
          bird or a rabbit with its eyes still closed,
              curled in a broad poem.
I am uncomfortable
with generosity,
          have no respect for fragility,
regularly mistake the heart's content
                for the whole of the heart's contents.
    This is why we can't have nice things.
    Why there are no signs of habitation.

No one deserves what they deserve.
I would like you to return to this landscape.
> If I rebuild the house from a blueprint of feathers.
> If to the specifications of memory on waking.
> I have a scrim we can light to the desired opacity.
> I will wear whatever costume does it for you.
> I am ordering a backdrop that looks good
> with your eyes.

ACTUAL ANIMALS

It's not that the antlers pain, exactly,
        budding from her forehead,
    but they do in the first few weeks
        feel raw,
    and her gait
            changes to accommodate
    the weight of them,
        so that she feels as if her head
           is still turning after
        it stops,
           and there are doorways
        to consider,
           and other people's eyes,
    so that after a while
           she stops coming inside,
        and watches the house
from the edge of the woods,
           thinking: those were my parents,
        but now they are just people,
    thinking once I slept there, and not
           in a swirl of grass.
She remembers the last
           boy she kissed longest
of all, but even that
        goes with time
           as her flank browns and dapples
        and she grows elegant, tentative,
           and dumb.

PRESUMED LOST

I write because I care. When I crossed you out,
it was for the better good. I hear the post office
is without two coins to pull from behind the ears

of children. No post stands forever. There is no sign
that won't spin. I write because I care. Some cares
have no analogue in the language I can chuff

from this throat. I have to scratch them into paper.
I write to you but there's no hope you'll see it.
Cholera on the trail. This horse founders. That horse shies.

The widow sells the farm, the farm hands,
and the orphan girl, too. This envelope glitters like a city
at night. There's no city here. No forwarding address.

No one to sign. The road folds up to a wadded letter.
I have been writing you for years to no avail. Happy Christmas.
Happy New Years. This year was a hard one. The chickens all died.

This year was rich and the grain spilt from our pockets.
The letters arrive in the post. The letters compressed
make a post. The house loses its roof. The house opens up

and we see ourselves inside, blithely reading. There is no way
to write my name next to yours without feeling a certain
sinking. I write because I care. I will ask the birds

to forward this. I will ask that a fox carry this missive farther. To where the real wild is. To where you make your home, outside the grid.

BRAID

I do not want to feel as I did,
                raw and tangential
to the world and its censure,
                humbled
                by the God in the grackle's gold piping,
                    the dividing and dying
                          cells in its black satin head.
I do not want to be the woman
        who cut off her hands
to see who'll love her after.

                When I shut my eyes
            I am still the same
                but you are disappeared. Thank God.
                          Thank God.

    Finally, he's crossed the right strand
            over the left,
                he's kept his fingers taut,
        and a solid cord
        forms from weaker threads.

I do not want to feel as I did,
                pinned under a heavier concern,
    your body
        responsible
            for my body,

        my body
      responsible
    for your body,

    the way your leg
       hooked over mine and we were locked in
           for the duration,

   the two of us ducking and covering
      over and around
until something greater formed, for a moment
        stronger than either of us.

IN THE GARDEN BEFORE THEY WERE ANIMALS

He holds his thumb to the pulse
               in her neck, presses.
I could make you lose consciousness, he said. *I could do that.*

                              She is not adverse,
                                    has no allegiance
                              to the ornamental pears
                          that burst into selected beauty
                     all around them, releasing the scent
                              of rotting meat—

The image of them in this garden,
        sprawled on the last grasses of summer
need not remain

                uncultivated,

                            though he is a wilderness,
                            though she is.

There are graftings that have taken.
There are careful prunings.

                            She might see this last gesture
                                as kindness, not a threat.

    I could, he is saying, *but I won't.*

When she shifts her position and her hair falls around
                his face—again the beauty
takes precedence
over any utility—
        he doesn't care
                if she shades his face
        from the sun, just that she is, for this last time, there.

THE DRESS LOOKS NICE ON YOU

The sounds I made are still falling
        over the small city, over the lake
                      glazed by sun
        and the boathouse's metal roof,
            over the trees full of grackles,
                of furled and future
                      breakage.

Before the glare and the blind
        in the earlier
                noon which was when all things
                or more things
                were possible,

he listened to my sounds, said
                      it's no good to lie ferocious in the debt
                      between love and love's withdrawals.
                      The world sees the world, even in the night.
                      Pull the stars out now. Paste the moon.
                      Let it all be very genuine.

Over the small city, the lake, the boathouse
        with the boats that never left dock,
these sounds he made
        also echo, echo too, there wasn't even one
                I've forgotten I carry them. I carry them.

BOUND LIKE ISSAC

Bound like a sheep, horizontal
                     pupil fixed
                     to the earth,
I have been unknowing and pliant,
     worse, I have walked meekly behind
the hand carrying the knife,
     worse, I loved that hand,
     even as it sharpened
     the blade, I pressed
               my muzzle
         to its unyielding,
               lipped at bitter grain
               and called myself fortunate.

Bound like a calf
               trussed by the legs,
bound like a child
     to a tree and left calling

for my friends—
they were not my friends—

I stepped to
     when whistled at, I put my arms
          behind my back, I told myself
there was a greater love

        that might step in,
and then later, when no voice sounded,
                I was the real alone, alone.

SELF PORTRAIT AS POST SCRIPT

And another thing
               another thing
        another thing spills out when I am a rose bush
             cascade of lyre bird spill out of plumage
these ancillary passages of peacock feather
these pumped out plush petals the plus
             of the bloom the minus of the bud
stacks of animals
    a still life studying
               the many pretty ways to die

if these swirling vines look like my hand
             please realize the black beyond I stand by
      is set to devour these words
                   your name
             one my syllable to swallow and lick
             one my sign off to the greater good

going down to where the downed and feathered
             flesh parts to a knife's
                  introduction to meat
symmetry in the cock's comb symmetry
       in the aureole the glands starring the nipple
and if the moles match the constellations
             if this sky was the same in your world
as in mine, which is as it was

                        when the giant squids
unfurled in the depths of dark
                        with the soft seaweed light
            squinted into a tube
such is the filigree of me
against the velvet
            my shy knees crossed against the
                        once again and never more.

Thanks to the following for publishing some of these poems in different forms: *New American Writing, Pleiades, Vinyl Poetry, Sixth Finch, Catch Up, Ink Node, Southern Indiana Review, Floating Wolf Press.*

Thank you to KMA Sullivan for choosing this book! And the wonderful staff at YesYes/*Vinyl!* Thanks to Brittany Cavallaro and Sean Bishop for their feedback on some of these poems, and to my poem-a-day compatriots.

Rebecca Hazelton is the author of *Fair Copy* (Ohio State University Press, 2012), winner of the 2011 Ohio State University Press / The Journal Award in Poetry, and *Vow*, from Cleveland State University Press. She was the 2010-11 Jay C. and Ruth Halls Poetry Fellow at the University of Wisconsin, Madison Creative Writing Institute and winner of the "Discovery" / *Boston Review* 2012 Poetry Contest. Her poems have appeared in *AGNI*, *The Southern Review*, *Boston Review*, *Best New Poets 2011*, and *Best American Poetry 2013*.

ALSO FROM YESYES BOOKS

If I Should Say I Have Hope by Lynn Melnick

Boyishly by Tanya Olson

The Youngest Butcher in Illinois by Robert Ostrom

I Don't Mind If You're Feeling Alone by Thomas Patrick Levy

Heavy Petting by Gregory Sherl

Panic Attack, USA by Nate Slawson

Man vs Sky by Corey Zeller

Frequencies: A Chapbook and Music Anthology, Volume 1
[SPEAKING AMERICAN BY BOB HICOK, LOST JULY BY MOLLY GAUDRY, AND BURN BY PHILLIP B. WILLIAMS PLUS DOWNLOADABLE MUSIC FILES FROM SHARON VAN ETTEN, HERE WE GO MAGIC, AND OUTLANDS]

VINYL 45s
A PRINT CHAPBOOK SERIES

Pepper Girl by Jonterri Gadson

Still, the Shore by Keith Leonard

Please Don't Leave Me Scarlett Johansson by Thomas Patrick Levy

No by Ocean Vuong

POETRY SHOTS
A DIGITAL CHAPBOOK SERIES

The Blue Teratorn by Dorothea Lasky
[ART BY KAORI MITSUSHIMA]

Toward What Is Awful by Dana Guthrie Martin
[ART BY GHANGBIN KIM]

My Hologram Chamber Is Surrounded by Miles of Snow by Ben Mirov
[IMAGES BY ERIC AMLING]

Nocturne Trio by Metta Sáma
[ART BY MIHRET DAWIT]

How to Survive a Hotel Fire by Angela Veronica Wong
[ART BY MEGAN LAUREL]

KMA SULLIVAN, PUBLISHER
JILL KOLONGOWSKI, MANAGING EDITOR
JOHN MORTARA, SOCIAL MEDIA EDITOR
ROB MACDONALD, DIRECTOR OF EDUCATIONAL OUTREACH
STEPHEN DANOS, EDITOR-AT-LARGE
HEATHER BROWN, ASSISTANT MANAGING EDITOR
TORY ADKISSON, ASSISTANT EDITOR
JOANN BALINGIT, ASSISTANT EDITOR
STEVIE EDWARDS, ASSISTANT EDITOR
RAINA FIELDS, ASSISTANT EDITOR
NAZIFA ISLAM, ASSISTANT EDITOR
AMBER RAMBHAROSE, ASSISTANT EDITOR
MARK DERKS, FICTION EDITOR, *VINYL POETRY*
PHILLIP B. WILLIAMS, POETRY EDITOR, *VINYL POETRY*
ALBAN FISCHER, GRAPHIC DESIGNER
THOMAS PATRICK LEVY, WEBSITE DESIGN AND DEVELOPMENT